Contents

Introduction — 1

Definition and Importance — 2

Why is Mental Health Important? — 4

Common Misconceptions about Mental Health — 5

Relaxation Methods — 10

The Importance of Self-Care — 14

The Importance of Social Networks for Mental Health — 18

When Professional Help is Necessary — 22

Conclusion — 26

Resources and Further Reading — 27

Introduction

Welcome to your ultimate guide to mental health! In a world that is becoming faster-paced and more complex, it is more important than ever to take care of our mental health. This guide offers you practical tips, exercises, and valuable information to improve your well-being and lead a fulfilling life.

What is Mental Health?

Definition and Importance

Mental health is a comprehensive term that describes our emotional, psychological, and social well-being. It is an essential part of our overall health and influences every aspect of our lives. Mental health determines how we think, feel, and act. It plays a crucial role in how we handle stress, relate to others, and make decisions in our daily lives.

Emotional Health encompasses the ability to recognize, understand, and regulate our feelings. It allows us to experience positive emotions such as joy and satisfaction while also being able to deal constructively with negative feelings like sadness, anxiety, and anger.

Psychological Health refers to our cognitive processes, including our thinking, perceptions, and beliefs. It influences how we solve problems, process information, and interpret ourselves and the world around us. Healthy psychological functioning enables us to think clearly, set realistic goals, and find creative solutions to challenges.

Social Well-being is the ability to build and maintain healthy and fulfilling relationships with others. It involves developing social skills, maintaining a supportive network, and experiencing a sense of connection and community. Social well-being helps us to give and receive support, which is particularly valuable during difficult times.

Why is Mental Health Important?

Mental health is crucial for several reasons:

1. Quality of Life: Good mental health significantly contributes to our quality of life. It enables us to enjoy life to the fullest, overcome challenges, and lead a fulfilling and productive life.

2. Physical Health: There is a close connection between our mental and physical health. Chronic stress and psychological burdens can lead to physical illnesses, including heart disease, diabetes, and a weakened immune system.

3. Relationships: Healthy mental states foster strong and positive relationships. People with good mental health can communicate better, resolve conflicts, and empathize with others.

4. Performance: Mental health affects our ability to work and learn effectively. It enhances concentration, creativity, and problem-solving skills, which are beneficial in both professional and personal life.

5. Coping Mechanisms: Stable mental health provides the tools and resilience to cope with the inevitable stresses and crises of life. It helps us to bounce back from setbacks and recover from difficult situations.

Common Misconceptions about Mental Health

Despite increasing awareness and education about mental health, many misconceptions and stigmas still surround this topic. These misunderstandings can prevent people from seeking the necessary help and support. It is essential to debunk these myths to foster better understanding and acceptance.

1. "Mental Health Only Affects People with Mental Illnesses"

A common misconception is that mental health is only relevant for people struggling with diagnosed mental illnesses. In reality, mental health affects every one of us. It is a vital part of our overall well-being and influences how we think, feel, and act, regardless of whether we have a specific diagnosis. Everyone can benefit from mental health-promoting measures, such as stress management techniques and self-care.

2. "Mental Health Problems are a Sign of Weakness"

Another frequent misconception is that admitting to mental health problems is a sign of weakness. In fact, it takes great courage and strength to recognize issues and seek help. Mental health is like physical health: anyone may need support at some point. The stigma that people struggling with their mental health are weak prevents many from getting the help they need.

3. "You Can Just Overcome Mental Health Problems"

Many people mistakenly believe that mental health problems can simply be overcome through willpower or a positive attitude. While a positive outlook can be helpful, mental illnesses are often complex and require professional treatment and support. Depression, anxiety disorders, and other mental illnesses frequently have biological, psychological, and social causes that need comprehensive and targeted treatment approaches.

4. "Therapy is Only for "Crazy" People"

Therapy is often associated with extreme mental illnesses or unstable individuals. In reality, anyone can benefit from therapy, regardless of the severity of their issues. Therapy provides a safe space to explore feelings and thoughts, learn coping strategies, and overcome personal challenges. Many people seek therapy to deal with everyday stress, relationship problems, or personal growth goals.

5. "Medication is the Only Solution for Mental Health Problems"

While medications can be effective in treating many mental illnesses, they are often just one part of a broader treatment plan. Therapy, lifestyle changes, social support, and other approaches also play crucial roles in treating and managing mental illnesses. A holistic approach that combines various treatment methods often yields the best results.

6. "Children and Adolescents Don't Have Mental Health Problems"

A widespread misconception is that children and adolescents cannot have serious mental health issues. In reality, young people can also suffer from mental illnesses such as depression, anxiety disorders, and other problems. Early intervention and support are essential to help young people develop healthy coping strategies and minimize long-term impacts.

7. "Mental Health Problems are Rare"

Another misconception is that mental health problems are rare and only affect a few people. In fact, mental health issues are widespread. According to the World Health Organization (WHO), about 1 in 4 people worldwide will experience a mental or neurological disorder at some point in their lives. Awareness of the prevalence of these issues can help reduce stigma and mobilize more support for those affected.

8. "People with Mental Illnesses are Dangerous"

This misconception significantly contributes to the stigma and discrimination faced by people with mental illnesses. The vast majority of people with mental illnesses are not violent and pose no danger to others. In fact, they are often victims of violence and abuse. It is important to break down prejudices and develop a realistic and empathetic perspective on people with mental illnesses.

9. "Once You Feel Better, Treatment is Over"

Many people believe that treatment for mental health problems can end once they feel better. In reality, maintaining mental health is an ongoing process. Even when symptoms improve, it is important to continue treatment, take preventive measures, and regularly work on one's mental health to avoid relapses.

Understanding and debunking these misconceptions is crucial for creating a supportive and open-minded environment for people with mental health problems. By breaking down these myths, we can help reduce stigma and make it easier for people to access the necessary help and support.

Overall, it is important to recognize that mental health is an integral part of our lives that requires continuous attention and care. By developing a better understanding and awareness of mental health, we can contribute to creating a more supportive and healthier environment for ourselves and others.

Relaxation Methods

In a world that is often hectic and stressful, relaxation methods are essential for maintaining our mental and physical well-being. These techniques help us reduce stress, find inner calm, and improve our overall quality of life. Here are some proven relaxation methods that you can integrate into your daily routine:

1. Breathing Exercises

Breathing exercises are simple yet highly effective techniques to calm the mind and relax the body. They can be performed anytime, anywhere, and require no special equipment.

Deep Abdominal Breathing: Sit or lie down comfortably. Place one hand on your abdomen and breathe deeply through your nose, allowing your belly to rise. Hold your breath briefly and then exhale slowly through your mouth. Repeat this for a few minutes to feel immediate relaxation.

4-7-8 Technique: Inhale through your nose for 4 seconds, hold the breath for 7 seconds, and then exhale slowly through your mouth for 8 seconds. This technique helps calm the nervous system and can be particularly helpful before bedtime.

2. Progressive Muscle Relaxation

Progressive Muscle Relaxation (PMR) is a technique where

different muscle groups are systematically tensed and then relaxed. This method helps reduce physical tension and promotes a deep sense of relaxation.

Step-by-Step Guide:

Lie down or sit comfortably.

Start with your toes: Tense the muscles for 5-10 seconds and then release.

Gradually work your way up the body, including calves, thighs, abdomen, chest, arms, hands, neck, and face.

Focus on how each muscle group feels when tensed and then relaxed.

3. Meditation

Meditation is an ancient practice aimed at calming the mind and enhancing awareness. There are various styles of meditation, but all share the goal of promoting inner peace and clarity.

Mindfulness Meditation: Sit in a comfortable position and focus on your breath. Notice how the air flows in and out of your body. Allow thoughts to come and go without holding onto them.

Guided Meditation: Use apps or online resources that offer guided meditations. These can be particularly helpful if you are new to meditation.

4. Yoga

Yoga combines physical poses, breathing exercises, and meditation to relax the body and mind. There are different styles of yoga, ranging from gentle and relaxing to vigorous and dynamic.

Hatha Yoga: A gentle style focusing on basic poses and slow

movements. Ideal for beginners and for relaxation.

Yin Yoga: A slower style where poses are held longer to promote deeper stretches and relaxation.

5. Mindfulness

Mindfulness means being fully present in the moment without judgment. It helps calm the mind and reduce stress.

Mindfulness in Daily Life: Integrate mindfulness into everyday activities such as eating, walking, or even brushing your teeth. Focus on your senses and the experience of the moment.

Body Scan: Lie down and focus on each region of your body, from your toes to your head. Be aware of how each area feels and release any tension.

6. Aromatherapy

Aromatherapy uses essential oils to promote relaxation and well-being. Scents like lavender, chamomile, and eucalyptus have calming properties.

Application: Use a diffuser to spread essential oils in the room, or apply diluted oils directly to the skin (e.g., on your temples or wrists). You can also add a few drops to a warm bath.

7. Music Therapy

Music Therapy uses the power of music to influence emotions and promote relaxation. Listening to calming music can help soothe the mind and lower stress levels.

Relaxation Music: Listen to gentle, soothing music, nature sounds, or specially curated relaxation playlists to create a calm atmosphere.

Active Music Making: Making music yourself, whether through singing or playing an instrument, can also have a deeply relaxing effect.

These relaxation methods offer a variety of approaches that you can try to find the techniques that work best for you. By regularly incorporating relaxation exercises into your daily routine, you can strengthen your mental health and lead a more balanced and satisfying life.

The Importance of Self-Care

What is Self-Care?

Self-care refers to the conscious actions that a person takes to promote and maintain their physical, emotional, and mental well-being. It encompasses a variety of activities and practices aimed at reducing stress, improving health, and enhancing overall quality of life. Self-care is not selfish; it is necessary to replenish one's resources and enhance the ability to be there for others.

Why is Self-Care Important?

Self-care plays a crucial role in maintaining both mental and physical health. Here are some reasons why self-care is so important:

Stress Reduction and Burnout Prevention:

Regular self-care activities help reduce stress and prevent burnout. Taking time for oneself can mitigate the effects of chronic stress and strengthen resilience.

Promotion of Physical Health:

Self-care includes physical activities, healthy eating, and adequate sleep. These practices support physical health and reduce the risk of illnesses and health problems.

Emotional Stability and Well-being:

Regularly attending to emotional needs can achieve emotional stability. Activities such as meditation, journaling, or maintaining social relationships can promote emotional balance.

Improved Relationships:

Taking good care of oneself enhances the ability to maintain healthy and supportive relationships. Self-care increases energy levels and emotional availability, positively impacting interactions with others.

Increased Productivity and Creativity:

Being well-rested and emotionally balanced can boost productivity and creativity. Breaks and self-care activities provide opportunities to recharge and approach tasks with fresh energy.

Self-Care Practices

There are many ways to integrate self-care into daily life. Here are some proven methods:

Physical Self-Care:

Regular Exercise: Activities such as walking, yoga, dancing, or sports help keep the body fit and relax the mind.
Healthy Eating: A balanced diet provides the body with

necessary nutrients and supports overall well-being.

Adequate Sleep: Good sleep is essential for regeneration and maintaining mental health.

Emotional Self-Care:

Journaling: Writing down thoughts and feelings can help process emotions and gain clarity.

Mindfulness Exercises: Meditation and mindfulness practices promote emotional balance and help stay present in the moment.

Therapy or Counseling: Professional support can help manage emotional challenges and gain personal insights.

Social Self-Care:

Maintaining Relationships: Spending time with family and friends and nurturing relationships fosters a sense of belonging and support.
Setting Boundaries: Knowing when to say "no" and respecting personal boundaries is an important aspect of self-care.

Mental Self-Care:

Hobbies and Interests: Taking time for activities that bring joy can help relax the mind and recharge energy.
Continued Learning: Learning new skills or advancing in an area of interest promotes mental well-being and personal development.

Challenges and Solutions

Self-care can sometimes be seen as unimportant or selfish, especially in a society that values productivity and constant availability. Here are some challenges and solutions:

Lack of Time: Integrating self-care into a busy schedule can be difficult.

Solution: Plan short breaks and small self-care rituals throughout your day.

Guilt: Many feel guilty when taking time for themselves.

Solution: Recognize that self-care is necessary to be there for others in the long term.

Lack of Awareness of Self-Care Practices: Some people do not know how to start with self-care.

Solution: Experiment with different methods and find out what works best for you.

Self-care is an essential part of a healthy and fulfilling life. By consciously investing time and energy in our care, we can improve our well-being, strengthen our resilience, and reach our full potential. It is important to view self-care as a necessity and regularly integrate it into our daily lives.

The Importance of Social Networks for Mental Health

Social networks play a central role in our lives and have a significant impact on our mental health. They encompass the relationships and connections we have with family, friends, colleagues, and the community. These networks provide not only emotional support but also practical help and a sense of belonging.

1. Emotional Support

Social networks offer emotional support, which is crucial for mental health. When we feel stressed, anxious, or down, conversations with friends or family members can provide comfort and encouragement.

Understanding and Empathy: Sharing our feelings and experiences with trusted individuals can bring understanding and empathy, reducing feelings of isolation.

Mood Improvement: Social interactions can help lift our mood and promote positive emotions. Laughter and shared activities with friends and family contribute to the release of endorphins.

2. Practical Support

Social networks also provide practical support, which can be extremely helpful in difficult times.

Help with Daily Tasks: Friends and family can assist with daily tasks such as childcare, household chores, or transportation, significantly reducing stress.

Resources and Information: Social networks can give us access to important information and resources, whether through professional networks, community organizations, or online forums.

3. Sense of Belonging

A strong social network contributes to a sense of belonging and social cohesion.

Community Feeling: Being part of a community can boost self-esteem and well-being. It helps us realize we are not alone and that others have similar experiences.

Identity and Purpose: Social networks can help us define our identity and find meaning and purpose in life by allowing us to take on roles and responsibilities within the community.

4. Coping Strategies and Resilience

Social networks promote the development of coping strategies and resilience.

Sharing Experiences: By sharing experiences and coping strategies, we can learn from others' challenges and solutions.

Support in Times of Crisis: In times of crisis, such as grief, illness, or professional difficulties, social networks provide crucial support that helps us overcome these challenges and emerge stronger.

5. Promoting Healthy Behaviors

Social networks can promote healthy behaviors and reduce bad habits.

Positive Social Pressure: Friends and family can encourage us to make healthy choices, such as regular exercise, healthy eating, and avoiding harmful substances.

Group Activities: Participating in group activities like sports teams, cooking clubs, or support groups can reinforce healthy habits and strengthen social bonds.

6. Challenges and Negative Influences

It is important to acknowledge that social networks can also present challenges and negative influences.

Negative Relationships: Conflicts, toxic relationships, or negative social pressure can harm well-being. It is important to recognize such influences and set boundaries or distance oneself from negative relationships if necessary.

Excessive Use of Social Media: While social media can help stay connected, excessive use can lead to isolation, anxiety, and decreased self-esteem. A conscious and balanced approach to social media use is advisable.

Practical Tips for Maintaining Social Networks

Building and Maintaining Relationships:

Active Listening: Actively listen and show interest in the needs and feelings of others.

Regular Contact: Stay regularly in touch with friends and family, whether through in-person meetings, phone calls, or messages.

Reliability: Be reliable and keep promises to foster trust and dependability in your relationships.

Participating in Community Activities:

Engagement: Get involved in community projects, clubs, or volunteer activities to meet new people and expand your social network.

Shared Interests: Find groups or activities that match your interests to share common experiences and form new friendships.

Dealing with Negative Influences:

Setting Boundaries: Learn to set clear boundaries and distance yourself from negative influences.

Self-Care: Pay attention to your mental health and take time for self-care when social interactions become overwhelming.

Conclusion

Social networks are an essential component of our mental health. They provide emotional and practical support, foster a sense of belonging, and help us develop coping strategies and resilience. By maintaining and consciously shaping our social networks, we can sustainably improve our well-being and quality of life.

When Professional Help is Necessary

Recognizing when professional help is necessary for mental health issues is crucial for timely and effective treatment. While self-care and support from friends and family can be beneficial, there are times when professional assistance is required to address serious mental health problems.

Signs That Professional Help is Needed

There are several signs and symptoms indicating that it might be time to seek professional help:

Persistent Sadness or Irritability:

If feelings of sadness or irritability persist for more than two weeks and interfere with daily activities, this could be a sign of depression or another mental disorder.

Overwhelming Anxiety or Worry:

Persistent and excessive anxiety or worry that disrupts daily life may indicate an anxiety disorder. If you constantly feel anxious or worried and these feelings impact your quality of life, consider seeking professional help.

Difficulty Managing Daily Tasks:

If simple daily tasks, such as going to work, taking care of family, or enjoying social activities, become overwhelming or impossible, it may signal a serious mental health condition.

Changes in Eating or Sleeping Habits:

Significant changes in eating or sleeping habits, such as overeating or loss of appetite, insomnia, or excessive sleeping, can indicate mental health issues.

Social Isolation:

Increasing isolation from friends and family and losing interest in social activities may be signs of depression or another mental health disorder.

Thoughts of Self-Harm or Suicide:

Thoughts of self-harm or suicide should always be taken seriously. If you have such thoughts, it is crucial to seek professional help immediately.

Substance Abuse:

Excessive use of alcohol or drugs as a coping mechanism for emotional pain may indicate an underlying mental health problem requiring professional treatment.

Uncontrollable Anger or Violence:

Frequent and uncontrollable outbursts of anger or violent

behavior can be a sign of mental health issues that need professional intervention.

Types of Professional Help

There are various types of professional support available depending on individual needs and the nature of the mental health problems:

Psychotherapy:

Talk Therapy: A therapist helps understand and change thoughts, feelings, and behavior patterns. Different approaches such as cognitive-behavioral therapy (CBT), psychodynamic therapy, and humanistic therapy can be used.

Family and Couples Therapy: These forms of therapy focus on dynamics within families or partnerships and help resolve communication and relationship issues.

Medication:

Antidepressants: Often used to treat depression and anxiety disorders.

Anxiolytics: Medications that help reduce anxiety.

Antipsychotics: Used to treat severe mental illnesses like schizophrenia.

Mood Stabilizers: Help in treating mood disorders such as bipolar disorder.

Inpatient Treatment:

In severe cases, a stay in a psychiatric hospital may be necessary to ensure intensive care and treatment.

Crisis Intervention:

Immediate help in acute crisis situations, often through

emergency hotlines or specialized crisis centers.

Support from Self-Help Groups:

Groups led by individuals with similar experiences offer support and exchange of coping strategies.

How to Seek Professional Help

Talk to Your Primary Care Physician:

A first step can be visiting your primary care physician who can provide an initial assessment and referrals to specialists or therapists.

Online Search Services:

Use online search services or directories to find therapists, psychiatrists, and self-help groups in your area.

Recommendations from Friends and Family:

Recommendations from trusted individuals can also be helpful in finding qualified professionals.

Insurance Information:

Check with your health insurance provider about covered services and professionals within your insurance network.

Recognizing the need for professional help and seeking it in a timely manner can make a significant difference in managing and treating mental health issues. It is important to understand that there is no shame in seeking help and that support and treatment options are available to help you lead a healthy and fulfilling life.

Conclusion

Thank you for reading this guide on mental health. It is my sincere aim to provide you with valuable information and practical tips to promote and strengthen your mental well-being.

I would like to share a personal experience with you: A few years ago, I experienced burnout myself. It was a challenging and difficult time that profoundly highlighted the importance of mental health and self-care for me. Through professional help, support from family and friends, and the implementation of self-care practices, I was able to find my path to recovery.

This experience motivated me to write this guide to help others take their mental health seriously and take the necessary steps to lead a balanced and fulfilling life. Remember, it is okay to seek help and take time for yourself. Your mental health is just as important as your physical health and deserves the same attention and care.

I hope that the information and strategies presented in this guide help you improve and maintain your mental health. Take time for self-care, seek support when you need it, and remember that you are not alone.

Resources and Further Reading

Books

"The Mindful Way Through Depression" by Mark Williams: This book offers insights and practical techniques to combat depression through mindfulness.

"The Little Book of Calm" by Paul Wilson: A compact guide filled with simple techniques to reduce stress and promote calmness.

Websites

National Institute of Mental Health (NIMH): www.nimh.nih.gov – Provides extensive information on mental health conditions and treatments.

Mind: www.mind.org.uk – Offers advice and support for anyone experiencing mental health issues.

Hotlines

National Suicide Prevention Lifeline (USA): 1-800-273-8255 – Provides free and confidential support for people in distress.

Samaritans (UK and Ireland): 116 123 – Offers emotional support to anyone in distress or struggling to cope.

9 798326 988393